PRE-INTERMEDIATE LEVEL

RACHEL BLADON

Gandhi

PRE-INTERMEDIATE LEVEL

Founding Editor: John Milne

The Macmillan Readers provide a choice of enjoyable reading materials for learners of English. The series is published at six levels – Starter, Beginner, Elementary, Pre-intermediate, Intermediate and Upper.

Level Control
Information, structure and vocabulary are controlled to suit the students' ability at each level.

The number of words at each level:

Starter	about 300 basic words
Beginner	about 600 basic words
Elementary	about 1100 basic words
Pre-intermediate	about 1400 basic words
Intermediate	about 1600 basic words
Upper	about 2200 basic words

Vocabulary
Some difficult words and phrases in this book are important for understanding the story. Some of these words are explained in the story, some are shown in the pictures, and others are marked with a number like this: …³. Phrases are marked with ᴾ. Words with a number are explained in the *Glossary* at the end of the book and phrases are explained on the *Useful Phrases* page.

Answer Keys
Answer Keys for the *Points for Understanding* and *Exercises* sections can be found at www.macmillanenglish.com/readers.

Audio Download
There is an audio download available to buy for this title. Visit www.macmillanenglish.com/readers for more information.

Contents

The Places In This Biography

South Africa in the late 1800s

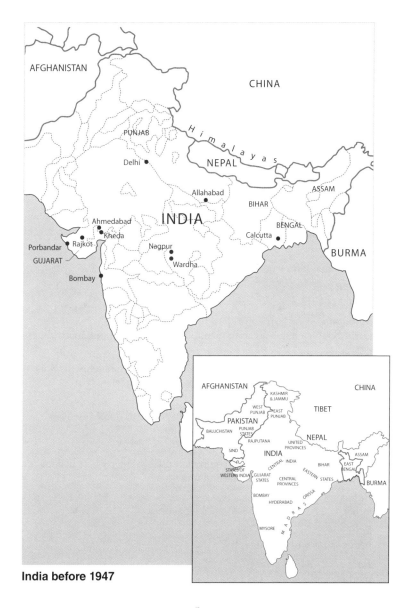

India before 1947

A Glossary Of Indian Terms

Raj
a Hindustani word for *rule* – the person, group or country that officially controls a place

diwan
first minister – an official who is in charge of a government department in the UK and in other countries

satyagraha
truth-force or love-force

swaraj
independence – freedom from control by another country or organization

ashram
a communal farm where people live and work together

harijan
a child of God

Mahatma
Great Soul – a name given to Gandhi by the poet Rabindranath Tagore

hartal
a general strike – a period of time during which people refuse to work and all businesses and services are closed as a protest

khadi
home-spun cloth – material produced by people at home, used for making things such as clothes and curtains

charkha
a spinning wheel – a piece of equipment used in the past for making a long thin fibre used for sewing and weaving

Bapu
father

lathi
heavy sticks with metal ends

Ba
mother

1

Life under the British Raj

Mohandas Karamchand Gandhi was born in Porbandar, in Gujarat, on 2nd October 1869. At that time, India was part of the British Empire – a group of countries and lands around the world that were ruled[1] by Britain. The British made India's laws and the head of the Indian government[2] was the British Viceroy in Calcutta. This time of British rule was called the Raj, which means 'rule' in Hindustani, one of the many languages of India.

The British East India Company had first come to India at the beginning of the seventeenth century, when it was ruled by the Moghul Emperor[3] Jahangir. The British East India Company was a big, important organization that worked in Asia trading – buying and selling things like cotton, tea and silk[4]. The Portuguese and Dutch had arrived in India before the British and they had taken parts of it. But early in the seventeenth century the British fought against Portugal and the Dutch Republic – now the Netherlands – and won these parts of India for themselves. In 1670, King Charles II of England changed the rules of the British East India Company so that it could keep an army, fight wars and take new land. During the eighteenth century, the Moghul emperors began to lose power[5] in India. So the British East India Company fought many battles and began to take control[6] of larger areas.

By the 1850s, the British East India Company controlled most of India. But in 1857, Indian soldiers fought against their British commanders and there was a mutiny: the Indian soldiers refused to do what they were told[p]. The British had to send more soldiers to India to control the mutiny. When they

7

stopped the fighting in 1858, Britain took control of India. It became a colony[7] which was ruled by Queen Victoria of England.

Many people in India were very unhappy with British rule in the second half of the nineteenth century. Britain ruled large areas of the colony directly, but there were also more than five hundred princely states. These states were carefully controlled by the British, but ruled by Indian princes. After the mutiny of 1857, the British government took a lot of money and land from the rich people of India.

They also took a lot of money in taxes[8] from Indian peasant[9] farmers, who were already very poor. They used this money to try and make India more modern – they built schools, law courts[10], roads, railways and bridges. Although Indians were pleased to use the things the British built, all the best jobs were given to the British. Many Indian people also felt that life was changing too fast. Some were worried that the British would make them change their religion and become Christians.

There were other problems for Indian people living under British rule too. There was a lot of illness and India also had some terrible famines – times when there was no food for people to eat. During the Great Famine of 1876 to 1878, up to ten million people died. Many Indian people believed these famines happened because of the way the British ruled India.

The areas of India that were ruled directly by Britain were very different from the princely states, which did not change and become modern so quickly. The princely states were very different from each other too. Some were richer and bigger than others, and the rulers had many different religions. There was often fighting between them.

India was also divided[11] by the caste system, which forced[12] society[13] into different groups. There were four main castes – the Brahmins, the Kshatriyas, the Vaishyas and the Shudras – with many smaller groups in each one. In the old Hindu

Indians waiting on the British Raj

caste system, people from each caste could only do certain jobs, so the Brahmins were teachers and religious leaders[14], the Kshatriyas were rulers and soldiers, the Vaishyas were traders and farmers and the Shudras were poor workers. Only people from the higher castes had political[15] power and nobody usually married outside their caste. At the bottom of society there were the Untouchables, who did difficult, dirty or dangerous jobs and lived in terrible conditions[16]. They were kept away from people from the other castes.

The people of India also had different religions. Hinduism was the main religion, but about a quarter of Indians were Muslims. There were also people of many other religions, including Parsis, Christians, Buddhists and Sikhs. Indian Hindus and Muslims usually lived very different lives and there were sometimes bad feelings between the two religious groups. In the early days of British rule, some Muslims refused to learn

English and work with the English government, so Hindus had better jobs in the Raj and this often caused problems.

Indians also spoke different languages. Bombay – now called Mumbai – was western India's biggest city and most people there spoke Marathi. The Viceroy ruled from Calcutta in the east, where Bengali was the main language. And in the old city of Delhi, hundreds of miles to the north, most people spoke Hindustani. Many other languages were also spoken in India.

So by the late nineteenth century, India was divided in many ways and many Indians were ready for change. In 1885, a group of lawyers[17], doctors and other educated people from different parts of India started a new political party, the Indian National Congress. They wanted educated Indians to have a more important part in governing their country. At first, they were not asking for independence[18] for India. However, after a few years, when the British government did not give them what they had asked for, 'The Congress' began to change and turned against British rule.

2

Young Gandhi

Porbandar, where Mohandas Karamchand Gandhi was born, was a quiet seaside town on the north-west coast of India, and the Gandhi family lived in a large old house on the edge of the town. They were a cultured Hindu family – they had books in their home and Mohandas played music when he was young. The Gandhis were part of the Vaishya caste. It was not a high caste, but the Gandhis had more money than a lot of Indian families. By the late nineteenth century, people's jobs were not always decided by their caste and Mohandas' father, Karamchand, was an important man. He was a diwan – or first minister – of the princely state of Porbandar, so he helped to rule the state. He was brave[19], generous and honest, but easily got angry. Mohandas' mother, Putlibai, was an intelligent, sensible[20] woman and Mohandas loved her very much. She was very religious. She prayed[21] before every meal and went to the temple every day. Like many Hindus, she also often fasted – she ate and drank nothing for several days.

Mohandas was the youngest of four children. He started school in Porbandar, but when he was seven years old, Karamchand got a new job in the city of Rajkot, 120 miles east of Porbandar, so the Gandhis moved.

At his primary school in Rajkot, Mohandas was not one of the best students, but he always arrived early. If breakfast was not ready in the morning, he ate food from the day before so he would not be late. He was a shy[22] boy and he was very frightened of ghosts, robbers and snakes[23]. He had to have a light on in his bedroom at night and he did not like to go anywhere in the dark.

After primary school, Mohandas went to Rajkot's Alfred High School, where his lessons were all in English. In his first year there, Mohandas showed that he already had a very honest nature. A British official[24] came to visit the school and Mohandas' class were asked to spell five English words. Mohandas wrote 'kettle' wrongly, so the teacher told him to copy the right spelling from another child. But Mohandas refused.

The children at Alfred High School were Muslim, Hindu and Parsi. Gandhi later said that he had first seen at school how important it was for people of different religions to live together peacefully[25]. He was interested in religion and when his father talked with his many Muslim and Parsi friends, Mohandas enjoyed listening to them and learning about their different beliefs. But he did not believe in God at that time and he stayed away from the Hindu temple.

Mohandas disliked all the rules that came with religion. Because of his mother's strong Hindu beliefs, and the Jain[26] traditions[27] of the area where his family lived, there were many rules in Mohandas' home. The family were not allowed[28] to touch or eat meat. This meant that Mohandas could not become a doctor, because student doctors had to cut up animals.

When Mohandas was only twelve, Putlibai told her children that they must not touch Uka, the 'Untouchable' boy who cleaned the toilets in their house in Rajkot. If they came close to an Untouchable by mistake, Putlibai told them, they had to have a bath. Mohandas argued with his mother about these rules, but he tried to do what she told him.

Mohandas had been a very shy boy, but when he got older he made some good friends and often played with them in the streets. He also enjoyed reading and liked going to see plays. Mohandas went to see a play about Harishchandra, a king in Hindu history who never told lies and always kept his promises. In the play, Harishchandra had to sell himself and his wife and son, and they suffered[29] terribly. Mohandas was very moved[30] by the play, which made him cry, and he acted it out to himself many times.

In 1883, when he was still only thirteen years old, Mohandas married Kasturbai Makanji Kapadia, who was just a few months older than him. At the time, he was excited about the wedding because he enjoyed wearing special clothes and having great dinners with music and processions[31]. But his first years with Kasturbai were very difficult. When she wanted to go out, she had to ask him. He often said no, but she still went. She often ran away to see friends and family without telling him and she did not let Mohandas teach her English and maths. And while Mohandas was still frightened of ghosts, robbers and snakes, and could not sleep without a light, Kasturbai was frightened of nothing. Often they did not speak to each other for several days. But Mohandas still loved Kasturbai.

When Mohandas was fourteen, he became friends with a boy called Mehtab. Mehtab was very different from Mohandas: he was very brave. Mehtab told Mohandas that this was because he ate meat. He also said that many of their teachers ate meat secretly and that if all Indians ate meat, they could fight against the British and make India free. Every day Mehtab tried to make Mohandas eat meat and at last Mohandas agreed. The two boys met in a quiet place and Mehtab brought some cooked goat's meat with him. Mohandas ate it and was sick at first. But they met several more times and Mehtab brought more meat. Mohandas ate it, but he felt guilty and did not like telling lies. After about a year, he stopped eating meat and decided not to eat it again while his parents were alive.

When Mohandas was sixteen and Kasturbai was expecting their first child, Mohandas' father became very ill. Mohandas helped to care[32] for him every night. One night, Mohandas' uncle came to care for Karamchand, so Mohandas went to bed. But a short time later, Karamchand died. For the rest of his life, Gandhi was always very sorry that he had not been with his father when he died. Soon after Karamchand's death, Kasturbai had a baby which died after just a few days. It was a very sad time for Mohandas.

After Mohandas left high school, he went to Samaldas College in Bhavnagar for a time. But he was not happy there and a friend of the family said he should go to England and study law. Mohandas wanted to go very much, but his mother was worried. How would the family pay for it? And would Mohandas forget about their religious rules? Finally, Mohandas' brother said that he would pay for Mohandas to go to London. Mohandas also took three vows[33] before a Jain monk[34]. He promised not to touch wine, women or meat. Then Putlibai agreed that Mohandas could go.

In September 1888, Mohandas bought a jacket and tie, some sweets and fruit, and sailed from Bombay to Southampton in England. A few months before, his first son, Harilal, had been born. Mohandas was still only eighteen years old.

3

London

The journey to England was not easy for Gandhi. He found it difficult to speak in English and he felt very nervous around the other people on the boat. Because of his promise not to have meat, for most of the journey he ate only the sweets and fruit that he had brought with him. When the boat arrived in England, Gandhi put on a white suit. But he found that no one else was dressed like him.

Gandhi stayed at a hotel for his first few days in London. But an Indian friend of his family told him that he should find a room with an English family to learn about the way English people lived. Gandhi did what the friend suggested and found a room in a family house. But for his first few months in London, he was terribly homesick – he missed his own family, and he found everything in England very strange. And because he could not eat meat and could not find vegetarian food at first, he was often hungry too.

Then one day, Gandhi found a vegetarian restaurant in London. He went in and enjoyed his first good meal since arriving in England. While he was there, he bought a book about vegetarianism. After he had read the book, he decided vegetarianism was a very good way to live. So from this time on, he was no longer a vegetarian because of his promise to his mother. He was a vegetarian because he believed in vegetarianism.

Gandhi began to enjoy London more, and for a while he decided to become 'an English gentleman'. He bought expensive suits, hats and ties, and spent ten minutes every morning combing his hair. He took lessons in dancing, French and the violin, and he learnt to speak properly in English.

But after about three months, Gandhi decided to live a simpler life. He could see that these lessons would not make him into[P] an English gentleman. He began to understand that it was more important to be strong inside than to look and sound right, so he stopped the dancing, French and violin lessons.

Gandhi as a law student

15

Gandhi did well in his law studies and while he was in London, he learnt a lot about other things too. When he was a second year law student, he read the Bhagavad Gita – the most important book in Hinduism – for the first time. The Bhagavad Gita became very important for Gandhi for the rest of his life. He also read the Bible and books about Buddhism. He believed now that there was a God, but he was still trying to decide which religion he should follow.

In his second year in England, Gandhi also travelled to Paris for the World Exhibition. The late nineteenth century was a time when European countries were very proud of the way they had changed and become modern. At the World Exhibition, the French showed many new buildings they had put up in Paris. One of these buildings was the Eiffel Tower, and Gandhi went up it two or three times.

In the summer of 1890, Gandhi went to the International Vegetarian Congress in London, a big meeting for vegetarians, and he was then asked to join the executive committee[35] of the London Vegetarian Society (LVS).

Gandhi's work with British vegetarians introduced him to politics. He had to organize meetings, speak at them and find people to give money to the LVS. He wrote nine articles for the LVS's publication[36] *The Vegetarian* between February and April 1891, and he also started a vegetarian club in London. He was still nervous when he had to speak in front of people, but he was learning things which would be very useful in his later life.

Gandhi passed his law exams and was 'called to the bar' – made a barrister – on 10th June 1891. Two days later, he sailed for India.

When Gandhi arrived home, his brother met him in Bombay. He had some terrible news for Gandhi. Their mother, Putlibai, had died soon after she had heard that her son had passed his exams. Gandhi had loved his mother deeply and he was filled with terrible sadness at this news. When they arrived in Rajkot, the family home was newly painted to welcome the homecoming barrister. Gandhi was pleased to be home with his family. His life with Kasturbai was difficult at first, but they became closer and in October 1892, their second son, Manilal, was born. But Gandhi could not find work. He moved to Bombay for six months but still did not get a job. And back in Rajkot, he had an argument with a British official, which made life there very difficult for him[p]. He had been without work for nearly two years. So when a law firm in South Africa invited him to work there for a year, Gandhi felt he had to go.

4

South Africa

When Gandhi arrived alone in South Africa in May 1893, he found that it was deeply divided. The Dutch and British had come to South Africa in the seventeenth and eighteenth centuries. They had taken land from the black people who had lived there for thousands of years and made those people into servants[37]. In 1893, South Africa was divided into four parts: Natal, which was ruled by the British; the Cape, a British colony which had its own government; and the Transvaal and Orange Free State, which were both ruled as independent countries by Dutch farmers called the 'Boers'.

There were many different people in South Africa at that time: white people with different languages and different ideas, and many groups of black people who had different religions and languages and lived in different ways. There were also groups that were referred to as 'coloured people' – Asians who the Dutch had brought to South Africa to work for them –

17

and, from 1860, Indians. Some Indians were brought to South Africa by the British to work on farms as 'indentured[38] workers' for five years and others – 'free Indians' – came to buy and sell things there.

In the Transvaal, for example, there were 650,000 black people, 120,000 whites and about five thousand Indians. The whites did all the important jobs and behaved very badly towards the Indians and blacks. In some parts of South Africa, Indians and blacks were not allowed to walk on pavements and they could only go out in the evenings if they had a letter from their boss. In other parts, they were not allowed to own land or buy or sell things.

Gandhi had come to South Africa to work and make some money. But he quickly found out what life there was like for Indian people – or 'coolies', as the British called them. Gandhi's boat from India had arrived in Durban, in Natal, and he had to make a long overnight journey from there to Pretoria, in the Transvaal, where he was going to work. Gandhi was given a first class train ticket for the first part of the journey, but when he sat in the first class area, two rail officials told him to move to third class.

'But I have a first class ticket,' Gandhi replied. He refused to move seats, so the officials called a policeman. Gandhi was taken off the train, and that night, he had to stay in a cold, empty station. Gandhi could not believe what had happened and he lay awake thinking. Should he go back to India now? Should he finish his work and then go back? Or should he stay in South Africa and fight against this kind of prejudice[39]?

The next morning, Gandhi spoke to other Indian people who told him more terrible stories about the way whites behaved towards them. For the next part of his journey, he had to travel by stagecoach, and because he was Indian he was not allowed to sit inside. He did not argue against this, but when a stagecoach official told him to sit on the floor, he refused. The official then began hitting him and tried to push him out of the stagecoach until some of the other passengers stopped him.

On the next train that Gandhi had to take, he was again told to move to the third class area by a rail official. This time, an Englishman in the first class area told the official to go away and Gandhi was able to use his first class ticket.

This journey from Durban to Pretoria changed Gandhi's life. A week after arriving in Pretoria, Gandhi asked all the Indians in the town to come to a meeting, where he made his first public speech. He wanted to talk to the Indian people about their lives and ways of improving them. The meetings continued and Gandhi soon knew every Indian in Pretoria.

Gandhi's work for the law firm in Pretoria went well and he learnt a lot about the law. He learnt other things during his year in Pretoria too. He met many Christians and read books about Christianity and other religions. Many of the people he met wanted him to become a Christian or a Muslim, but Gandhi was beginning to believe that Hinduism was the right religion for him.

He also read many other books during his year in South Africa, including works by the Russian writer Leo Tolstoy, who had many important ideas which interested Gandhi. Tolstoy had been born into a rich, important family, but when he was nearly sixty, he began living a simpler life. He farmed with the peasants, stopped eating meat and started wearing simple clothes. He believed he should live as his religious beliefs told him to. Gandhi said that Tolstoy's *The Kingdom of God is Within You* moved him deeply and taught him that violence was wrong.

When Gandhi had finished his work in Pretoria and was in Durban getting ready to sail back to India, he heard some important news. At that time, free Indians in Natal could vote[40], but the government there was planning to introduce a new law that would take away the Indians' vote. Gandhi's friends asked him to stay and fight against the new law and he agreed to stay in Durban for another month. He wrote many letters arguing against the new law and he organized petitions – long lists where people wrote their names to show they did not agree.

The petitions and letters did not stop the government and the new law was introduced, but something special was beginning to happen among the Indians in South Africa. Indians of different religions – Muslims, Hindus, Parsis and Christians – and Indians who had many different kinds of job all helped Gandhi with his letters and petitions. They were beginning to work together to try and improve their lives. Gandhi had promised to stay in South Africa for another month, but the Durban Indians now asked him to stay for longer. They knew that they needed his help and Gandhi knew it too. He agreed to stay, found a house in Durban and said that he would work as a barrister for the Indian people.

In May 1894, Gandhi and some of his friends set up[41] a political party, the Natal Indian Congress (NIC). They did this just in time, as there was another difficult change to come for the Indian people of Natal. Some of the indentured workers who had finished their five years on farms had decided to stay in South Africa and work there. The whites were worried about this and wanted the Indians to return home, so a new tax was put on any Indian who stayed in Natal after the end of his indenture. And because the tax was the same as six months' pay for an indentured worker, Indians, with Gandhi and the NIC behind them, were furious[42] about it.

By 1896, Gandhi had become a very good barrister and an important person in Indian politics in South Africa. He spoke at many meetings, organized lots of petitions and wrote letters to newspapers about the difficulties of life for Indians in South Africa. He also made many friends – Indians, whites and blacks – and he could talk easily with both the poorest and most important people he met. He had shown that he was

Gandhi working as a young lawyer in South Africa

extremely hard-working. He understood that white people were nervous because there were so many more Indians and black people than whites in South Africa. But because India was part of the British Empire, he wanted the laws the British made in South Africa to be the same for Indians and white people. Gandhi knew that whites would always be treated[43] better than Indians. But he hoped that if South Africa's laws were fair, Indian people's lives would slowly start to improve.

5

Satyagraha in South Africa

In 1896, Gandhi decided to return home to India for six months. While he was there, he spent a lot of time writing and talking at meetings about the way Indians were treated in South Africa. When he arrived back in Natal, bringing his family with him, another boat from India arrived by chance at the same time. There were eight hundred free Indians on the two boats. South African whites, who had read in newspapers about Gandhi's meetings in India, were furious. They believed that Gandhi was trying to fill Natal and the Transvaal with Indian people.

When Gandhi got off the boat, white people threw stones and eggs at him. Men kicked him and hit him. Gandhi was only saved when the wife of an important Durban policeman saw him. She knew Gandhi and she stood between him and the white men, keeping him safe. Gandhi was badly hurt, but he chose not to bring a law case against his attackers. It was not their fault, he said. It was the fault of the Natal government.

Because Gandhi decided not to bring a law case against his attackers, the difficult relationship between whites and Indians in Natal improved a little. A new law also helped. It gave the vote to anyone from the British Empire, including Indians, who could pass a special school test. So free Indians from Natal could vote once more.

Gandhi moved back into his house in Durban with Kasturbai, their two sons and a nephew they had brought with them from India. Gandhi made a lot of money from his work, but he also enjoyed helping people when they were ill. He had always wanted to be a doctor, and now he often helped at a dispensary[44] where he met many indentured workers.

In 1899, there was a war between the Dutch and British people of South Africa – the Boer War. Gandhi did not like war, but he could see that if the Indian people fought for the British, it might help them to improve their lives in South Africa.

At first, because of their prejudice against 'coloured people', the Natal government did not want the Indians' help. But after a while, they allowed them to set up the Indian Ambulance Corps, and more than a thousand Indians joined. Gandhi and his men worked very hard, taking soldiers to hospital and often walking up to forty kilometres a day. They were a great help to the British, and Gandhi and many others were given medals[45] for their brave work.

In 1902, when the war was over and the Transvaal and Orange Free State had become British colonies, Gandhi set up a law office in Johannesburg. Here, Gandhi began to live in a very simple way. For some time, he had cleaned his own bathroom and made his family do the same. This was unusual, because in Hindu homes the bathrooms were normally cleaned by Untouchables. Now Gandhi began to cut his own hair, wash his own clothes and eat a diet of fruit and nuts.

In 1903, Gandhi read a book by the poet, artist and social thinker John Ruskin, which changed his life. Ruskin said that people should try and find happiness from simple things in life, not from money. He also believed that rich people should take fewer things for themselves so that there was enough for the poor. After Gandhi had read Ruskin's book, he decided that he and his family would live on a farm. He bought a farm in Phoenix, near Durban, and built some simple houses there.

From 1904 to 1906, Gandhi and his family – he now had two more sons, Ramdas and Devadas – lived for part of the time in Johannesburg, near his law office, and for part of the time in Phoenix. There were always friends staying with the Gandhi family in Johannesburg. Gandhi liked everyone in the house to do as many things for themselves as they could. Gandhi also began to fast a lot, like his mother. He believed that his body should have only what it needed, and not what it wanted.

By 1906, Indian people in South Africa thought of Gandhi as their leader. That year, the government of the Transvaal decided to introduce a new law to make all Indian people carry[46] a pass – a paper that showed that an Indian person was allowed to stay in the Transvaal. Under the new law, anyone who did not have a pass had to pay a fine[47], go to prison or leave the Transvaal. The Indians were furious, and on 11th September 1906, Gandhi called a meeting in a theatre in Johannesburg. Nearly three thousand people came to the meeting.

Gandhi told the people at the meeting that he would prefer to die than carry a pass. He promised before God that he would not obey[48] the new law. As Hindus and Muslims, Gandhi said, Indians could not break a promise to God. So they should only make the promise if they were sure they were strong enough to keep it. And if just a few of them were strong enough, Gandhi went on, he was sure that they would win their fight. When they heard this, every person in the theatre stood up and promised before God that they would not obey the new law.

This was something very different and Gandhi decided that he needed a name for the idea of fighting peacefully against something by not obeying. He called it 'satyagraha', meaning truth-force or love-force. His followers, or 'satyagrahi', had to be strong inside themselves, Gandhi said. They had to get what they wanted by being honest.

In July 1907, the Transvaal government's new law – called the 'Black Act' by Indians – was introduced. Some Indians went to get their passes, but most did not, and in January 1908, Gandhi and other Indians who did not have passes were sent to prison. Gandhi was happy in prison and he spent a lot of time reading the Bhagavad Gita, the Bible and the Koran, as well as books by Ruskin, Leo Tolstoy and others. But on 30th January, General Smuts, one of the most important people in the Transvaal government, called Gandhi to meet with him. He said that if Indian people went freely to get their passes, he would repeal[49] the Black Act.

Many Indians were not happy about this and they didn't believe that Smuts would really repeal the law. But Gandhi argued that a satyagrahi had to trust people. He went to get his pass and many Indians followed him, but General Smuts did not repeal the Black Act. Because General Smuts had broken his promise, nearly two thousand Indians burnt their passes at a meeting in Johannesburg in August 1908.

Gandhi knew that a big fight against the Transvaal government was coming. His law office in Johannesburg became a 'satyagraha office' and he also spent a lot of time at his Phoenix farm, trying to get help from Natal Indians. Many important people openly gave Gandhi their help and Indians in South Africa and India, as well as many European South Africans, gave money to the satyagrahi. Everyone could see that the government was using the Black Act to stop Indian people from coming to live in the Transvaal. So satyagrahi began crossing from Natal into the Transvaal without passes. Many, including Gandhi, were sent to prison several times. At one time, 2,500 of the Transvaal's thirteen thousand Indians were in prison. They wanted to show the government that they would not obey its law.

Life was difficult for the families of satyagrahis who were in prison, so in 1910, a rich friend of Gandhi's, Hermann Kallenbach, bought a farm for them. Gandhi named it Tolstoy Farm after the writer whose work he so loved. On the farm, satyagrahis and their families made their own bread, marmalade and coffee. They also learnt to make shoes and wooden furniture. People slept on the ground, were not allowed to drink or smoke and had to walk if they wanted to go anywhere. The children were all taught on the farm by Gandhi and Kallenbach.

In 1911, Gandhi met with General Smuts. Smuts was now one of the leaders of the new Union of South Africa, which in 1910 had brought all four colonies of South Africa together into one dominion[50]. Smuts promised that he would make changes for the Indian people in South Africa, and so Gandhi agreed that satyagraha would stop. In October 1912, Gopal Krishna Gokhale, an important person in Indian politics, came to visit South Africa. He travelled around the country and met with General Smuts and the Prime Minister[51], General Botha, who promised Gokhale that they would allow Indian immigration[52]. They also said that they would no longer tax indentured workers who wanted to stay in South Africa.

But Smuts and Botha did not remove the tax on indentured workers and this made Indians angry. In March 1913, Indians became even angrier when the law court in Cape Colony said that Christian marriages were the only legal marriages in South Africa. Satyagraha started again, and this time many women joined too. Five thousand miners[53] went on strike[54] in Newcastle, Natal, and Gandhi told them to march[55] to the Transvaal. Gandhi was sent to prison and the miners were taken by train back to their mines, but satyagraha kept growing and growing. About fifty thousand indentured workers went on strike. Many people sent money for the satyagrahis, and in India and Britain there was great anger against the South African government.

When Gandhi got out of prison, he planned another march for January 1914. But when white workers from the South African railways went on strike, Gandhi said that he would cancel[56] the satyagrahis' march. He did not want to use satyagraha to break the government, he explained. He just wanted the government to give Indians back everything they had lost.

Marching to the Transvaal, November 1913

Because Gandhi had cancelled the satyagrahis' march, it became easier for Gandhi and Smuts to talk. They began to meet, and in July 1914, a new law was introduced. The new law said that Hindu, Muslim and Parsi marriages were legal. It did not allow Indians to move from one part of South Africa to another, but it removed the tax on indentured workers. The Indian people had not won everything they wanted, but most people were pleased with the law. Importantly for Gandhi, he had shown that satyagraha was a powerful force which could help to change things in other parts of the world too.

On 18th July 1914, Gandhi began his long journey home to India, via England, with Kasturbai and his family. He had come to South Africa for one year and had stayed for over twenty. His satyagraha campaign[57] had helped to win back for the Indian people many of the rights[58] that had been taken from them.

6

Back to India

When Gopal Krishna Gokhale had visited South Africa in 1912, he spoke a lot with Gandhi about Indian politics and problems. Gokhale believed that Gandhi could help India and he wanted him to come back to his homeland soon. When Gandhi's ship arrived in Bombay in January 1915, many people came to welcome him home. But outside Bombay, Calcutta and Gujarat, few people knew about Gandhi and he knew very little about India.

Gandhi began to travel around the country by train, meeting lots of people and talking about his ideas of 'swaraj', or independence, for India. Gandhi wanted Britain to leave India, but he liked Britain and did not think of the British as India's enemy. He believed that if Indians behaved fairly towards Britain, their country would soon become free.

When Gandhi had left South Africa, he was still wearing European clothes, but he now began dressing in simple Indian clothes. He spoke at meetings in a quiet voice and many people were very disappointed[59] when they saw him. They could not believe that this small, quiet man could lead India to independence.

Gandhi told India's politicians that they had to go out among the people in the villages and speak to them in local languages, not English. More than eighty per cent of Indian people were peasants, who had little money and had often not been to school. Gandhi did not just want to free India from British rule. He also wanted to free India's peasants from their poor and uneducated lives. He believed that if Indian people could feel free inside, they could easily free themselves from British rule. Slowly, Gandhi's words began to touch India, and people started to see that their country could be strong and proud once more.

Gandhi in India, 1915

In May 1915, Gandhi set up an 'ashram' – a communal farm where people lived and worked together – near the town of Ahmedabad. The farm was called the Sabarmati Ashram and Gandhi lived there with his family, friends and other people who worked with them. There were about thirty people in the ashram at first, but later more than two hundred people lived there. Everyone on the ashram – the ashramites – had to make bread, spin[60] and weave to make cloth, and teach in the villages nearby. They also had to make many promises about the way they lived. One of the ashramites' promises was that they would not treat Untouchables differently from people of other castes.

But when an Untouchable family came to live in the ashram, Kasturbai and some of the other ashramites were very upset. They hated to see an Untouchable woman cooking in their kitchen. People outside the ashram were also shocked and stopped giving money to the ashram for a while. But Kasturbai and the others slowly saw that Gandhi's ideas about Untouchables were right. He called the Untouchables 'Harijans' – children of God – and many people followed his example by letting Untouchables come and work in their homes. But the Untouchables were still extremely poor and Gandhi knew that there was a lot more to do to improve their lives.

By 1916, people all around India were beginning to hear about a brave little man who lived like a poor man in an ashram and worked for the poor. People came in large numbers to see and hear him speak. Gandhi's friend, the great poet and writer Rabindranath Tagore, had given him the name 'Mahatma' – or Great Soul – and when people saw Gandhi, they wanted to touch his feet. They believed that the Mahatma cared about them, understood their difficult lives and could help them.

In December 1916, at a meeting of the Indian National Congress party in Lucknow, a poor peasant called Rajkumar

Shukla came to see Gandhi. He wanted Gandhi to visit his home in Champaran, in the Himalayas, where poor farmers rented[61] land from the British. The farmers were treated very badly by them and were making very little money.

Gandhi went to Champaran to help and stayed there for a year. He was asked to leave by the British and had to go to court when he refused. But thousands of peasants demonstrated[62] outside the court and the British could not control these crowds without Gandhi's help. The court case was dropped and, working with lawyers, Gandhi helped to change things for the Champaran farmers. More importantly, the peasants of Champaran had learnt to be brave and Gandhi had shown them that they had rights.

But Gandhi wanted to do more than help with these farming problems. He saw that life in the villages of Champaran was very hard, so he asked teachers and a doctor to come there. Gandhi, Kasturbai and others from the ashram opened primary schools in six villages and taught people to keep their families and homes clean and healthy.

While Gandhi was working with the people of Champaran, he was suddenly called back to Ahmedabad. There were problems in the mills[63] there, with workers complaining that they had to work too hard and were not paid enough money. Gandhi agreed with the workers and asked the owners of the mills to talk with them. When the owners refused to hold talks, Gandhi told the workers to go on strike. He made them promise that they would strike until the mill owners gave them what they wanted or held talks. For the first two weeks, thousands of workers came to meet Gandhi every day near his ashram, but after a while, Gandhi could see that they were worried about continuing with the strike. On 15th March 1918, Gandhi told the mill workers that he would fast until they won what they wanted with their strike. The mill owners did not want Gandhi to die, so three days after Gandhi had started his fast, they promised to hold talks with the workers. It was the first time that Gandhi won a political fight by fasting.

There were problems in other parts of India at the beginning of 1918 too. In Kheda, terrible rains had ruined[64] the peasants' crops[65] and they did not have enough money to pay land tax to the British government. Gandhi decided to use satyagraha to help the peasants and he told them not to pay their land tax. More than three thousand peasants promised not to pay, and after five months, the Raj agreed that it would not collect land tax from very poor peasants that year. With Gandhi's help, the poorest Indians had shown they could be strong against the British.

7

Non-cooperation and the Cloth Campaign

More than half a million Indians fought for Britain in the First World War between 1914 and 1918. So when the war ended, there was a strong feeling that Britain should give India something back. During the war, Edwin Montagu, the Secretary of State[66] for India, had said that there would be a move towards 'responsible government' in India as a part of the British Empire, which, people believed, meant that India would begin to rule herself.

But in March 1919, a new law, the Rowlatt Act, was passed in India. Under the new law, Indians could be arrested[67] without trial[68] for sedition – trying to make other people act against the government. Any Indian who was caught carrying a seditious paper had to go to prison for two years.

The Indian people were furious. They had fought for Britain in the war and they had hoped that they would soon rule their own country. But they were given the Rowlatt Act, not self-government.

Gandhi decided that India should have a 'hartal' – everything should shut down. On 30th March in Delhi, and a week later in other cities, shops stayed closed and no one went to work. Everyone followed the hartal, and in cities and villages all over India, crowds of thousands of people demonstrated against the Rowlatt Act. In most parts of India, the demonstrations were peaceful, but there was some violence and fighting, and Gandhi was very upset when he heard this.

13th April 1919 was a terrible day in the history of British rule in India. Two days earlier, a new British army leader, General Dyer, had arrived in Amritsar, in the Punjab. He said that he would not allow public meetings because he was worried about violence. But many people in the city did not know he had said this, and on 13th April, more than ten thousand Hindus, Muslims and Sikhs met at Jallianwalla Bagh. Jallianwalla Bagh was a place with walls around it, where public meetings were often held. The meeting had only just started when General Dyer arrived with his soldiers. They stood at the entrance to Jallianwalla Bagh, so that people could not escape, and began shooting[69]. More than three hundred people were killed and more than a thousand were injured.

At first, the British did not let Gandhi go to the Punjab after the shootings in Amritsar. But in October 1919, he was allowed to travel there to help organize an investigation[70] into the shootings. When he arrived in Lahore, the railway station was full of people who had come to see him – they felt that he was the only person who could help them fight against the British.

Because of the Rowlatt Act and the Amritsar shootings, more and more people wanted India to move towards self-government. There were other reasons why Indian people were angry with the British government. The war had made

The Amritsar shootings, 1919

prices in India very high and many people could not afford
to eat properly. There was also anger among Indian Muslims
because Britain and her allies[71] had taken away the power of
their religious leader, the Caliph.

Gandhi now introduced the idea of 'non-cooperation' –
refusing to help or work with the British government. He told
the British Viceroy that from 1st August 1920, Indians would
stop buying British cloth, going to British schools and courts,
and working for the British government. The non-cooperation
campaign was followed across the country. Lawyers stopped

working in the courts and people refused to vote in local elections[72]. Teachers and students left the cities and went to teach reading, writing and non-cooperation in the villages. People also stopped drinking alcohol, which was taxed heavily and therefore brought the British government money.

Gandhi travelled around the country, speaking at meetings where often more than a hundred thousand people came to hear him. At these meetings, he asked Indians to stop wearing foreign clothes and told them they should learn to spin and weave to make their own cloth. People then took off their foreign clothes and Gandhi collected them at the front and burnt them. Gandhi began spinning himself for half an hour every day and he later dressed only in a loincloth – a piece of cloth around his middle. As a result of the cloth campaign, hundreds of thousands of Indians began wearing 'khadi' – home-spun cloth.

In 1920, Gandhi began working closely with the Indian National Congress and at their meeting in December, he helped to change the party into a big organization with representatives[73] in every city and village. A new flag was designed for the party with a picture of the 'charkha' – or spinning wheel – on it. Before 1920, the Congress had been ruled by important rich men, but at the December meeting there were many poor people, and the most important speakers were middle-class Indians like Gandhi. At this meeting, Gandhi promised that if India followed peaceful non-cooperation, it would have self-rule in less than a year.

As well as travelling around the country in hot, uncomfortable trains, Gandhi wrote many articles for *Young India* and *Navajivan*, his two weekly publications. Crowds wanted to see him day and night, and to give himself some peace, he began to have a weekly day of silence, which he continued for the rest of his life. He only spoke on a Monday if something very important happened.

After a year of non-cooperation, the Congress had six million new members and Hindus, Muslims and Sikhs were working and living together more peacefully than ever before. But there was still no self-rule for India and the British now began to arrest political leaders and those who followed them. By January 1922, thirty thousand Indians had been arrested and many were treated very badly and hit. Many Indians wanted to fight against the British, but Gandhi still believed that non-violence was the only way forward for India.

The Congress had agreed to begin a campaign of civil disobedience – people in one part of the country, the area of Bardoli, would all refuse to pay taxes. But in February 1922, there was violence in the small town of Chauri Chaura, where a crowd of demonstrators killed twenty-two policemen. Gandhi was deeply upset by the news and he decided to cancel the civil disobedience campaign. Many people were disappointed about this and thought that it was the wrong decision. But Gandhi was worried that he would not be able to control the campaign and he could not allow violence.

At this time, British leaders in India began to call for Gandhi's arrest. Lord Reading, the new Viceroy, liked Gandhi and did not want to put him into prison. But most of the British government in India felt that Gandhi was too dangerous, and on Friday 10th March 1922, he was arrested and taken to Sabarmati prison. A week later, he was brought to court and charged[74] with writing three seditious articles in *Young India.* Gandhi told the judge that the charge was completely fair and that he should receive the hardest penalty[75].

The judge told Gandhi that he would go to prison for six years. When Gandhi was taken away from the courtroom, people fell at his feet, many of them crying. But Gandhi walked away smiling. He had always said that going to prison was an important part of non-cooperation. It was only in prison, he believed, that freedom could be won.

8

Waiting for the Fight

Gandhi was taken to Yeravda Prison in Poona, where he spent his time spinning, reading and writing. He was always happy in prison, but things outside Yeravda were not so peaceful. Hindus and Muslims had begun to disagree once more. Non-cooperation had almost stopped, and many lawyers and teachers had gone back to their courts and schools. There was disagreement in the Congress too. 'Pro-Changers', led by Motilal Nehru and CR Das, wanted to go against Gandhi's beliefs and enter local elections. They believed that they could try to improve life for Indians from inside the councils, and in 1922, they set up a Swaraj Party. But a group of 'No-Changers' thought they were wrong and wanted to continue with Gandhi's non-cooperation campaign. Both groups stayed in the Congress, but there were terrible arguments between them.

On 12th January 1924, Gandhi was taken to hospital with appendicitis[76], and because he did not get better quickly, the government decided to release[77] him from prison on 5th February. Gandhi went to stay at the seaside home of a businessman at Juhu, near Bombay, and there he heard about the disagreements in the Congress. At a Congress meeting in Ahmedabad in June, Gandhi found that many people no longer wanted to follow his ideas and he cried openly at the meeting. But because he did not want members of the Congress to fight against each other, he made an agreement with Nehru and Das. He allowed the Swarajists to enter local elections and they agreed that Congress members had to spin on the charkha.

Gandhi now moved away from politics for a while and

spent his time thinking about the problems between Hindus and Muslims. He wrote a long article in *Young India* about two of the main disagreements: Hindus did not like Muslims killing cows and Muslims were often upset when Hindus played loud music near their mosques at prayer time. But there were other problems between the two religious groups. Many Muslims believed that Hindus had quietly gone back to the Raj's courts, schools and councils while they had stayed away and followed non-cooperation.

In September 1924, there was violence between Hindus and Muslims in Kohat, in the north-west of India, and Gandhi decided to fast for twenty-one days at the home of one of his Muslim friends. Gandhi had been very ill with appendicitis, and since coming out of hospital, had been busy with the problems inside the Congress and between Hindus and Muslims. He was not strong and many people worried that this fast might kill him. It did not, but it also did not stop the disagreements between Hindus and Muslims.

Gandhi's friends wanted him to become president of the Congress in 1925 to keep the party together, and he agreed. He also spent a lot of time that year writing his autobiography, *Satyagraha in South Africa*, and continuing his campaigns for khadi and equality[78] for the Untouchables. He travelled around India once again and thousands of people came to see him. To many people, he was like God. At every meeting, Gandhi told people to start spinning. He believed that spinning could bring everyone in India together – rich and poor, village people and city people. He also believed that spinning helped to organize people, so they would be ready for civil disobedience. Gandhi said that all members of the Congress should wear khadi, and although some people did not like the idea at first, by the mid-1920s everyone who wanted independence for India was dressing in homespun cloth.

In November 1925, tired from his travelling, Gandhi fasted

Gandhi spinning cloth in Gujarat, 1925

for seven days and told people that he was going to have a year of 'political silence'. He wanted to stay at the ashram and he said that he would not travel or go to any meetings. In that year, 1926, he wrote, saw visitors and spent a lot of time with his friends and the children at the ashram. The ashramites had become Gandhi's family and everyone there called him 'Bapu', or Father. He expected everyone on the ashram to keep it and themselves perfectly clean, to work hard and to spin every day. But life there was very happy, and no one was frightened of Gandhi, who often helped out in the kitchens himself.

But while Gandhi always treated his ashram family with kindness and love, he was very hard towards his own sons. He sent many young men to England to study, but did not give his own sons a good education, and this upset them. Harilal, Gandhi's eldest son, had a difficult life, possibly because he did not feel loved by his father, who had so much love for everyone else. He began drinking, became a Muslim and wrote articles attacking his father. Harilal's children came to live with Gandhi and Kasturbai, but for many years he did not see or speak to his father.

After Gandhi's year of silence, he began travelling and going to meetings once more in 1927. Often, at meetings, he held up five fingers. One, he said, was equality for the Untouchables, the second was spinning, the third was keeping away from alcohol, the fourth was friendship between Hindus and Muslims and the fifth was equality for women. Gandhi's wrist[79] was non-violence. These things would free every Indian's body, Gandhi said, and give India her independence. There were often as many as two hundred thousand people at Gandhi's meetings. Sometimes he sat in front of them in silence until they became quiet, then put his hands together in prayer and left.

All this time, Gandhi was waiting for a chance to start a new campaign of non-cooperation. He became ill in March 1927 and had to rest for a while, but he was travelling again when he heard that the new British Viceroy, Lord Irwin, wanted to see him. Gandhi travelled for two days to get back to Delhi, where other important Indian political leaders had also arrived. But Lord Irwin had nothing to say. He just gave Gandhi and the others a paper which told them that the Simon Commission – a group of people from England led by Lord Simon – would travel around India in 1928. The commission would then suggest any political changes that were needed.

When people heard that there would be no Indians on the

Simon Commission, they were furious. Across the country, No-Changers, Swarajists, Liberals and members of the Muslim League – a party led by Jinnah which campaigned for the rights of Muslim people – all agreed not to help the commission. When it began to travel around India in February 1928, there were shouts of 'Simon, go back!' wherever it went. India was ready to fight again.

9
The Salt March

In 1922, Gandhi had wanted to start a civil disobedience campaign in Bardoli in Gujarat, but he had cancelled it because of the violence at Chauri Chaura. In 1928, he decided that the time was right for civil disobedience and that Bardoli was still the right place for it. The British had just increased[80] land taxes in the Bardoli villages and the peasants were very angry. They began a campaign of civil disobedience, and for four months, they did not pay their taxes. The government took away their land and animals, and put hundreds of people in prison, but the peasants stayed strong.

On 6th August, their non-violent campaign won. The government gave back the peasants' land and animals, let the campaigners out of prison and cancelled the increase in taxes. Civil disobedience had won in Bardoli and many in India now wanted a campaign across the whole country. But Gandhi had learnt to wait for the right time and the right place.

The Congress met in Calcutta in December 1928, and at that meeting, younger members Jawaharlal Nehru and Subhas Bose became important voices. They did not think it was enough for India to become a dominion and wanted the country to be completely independent. Gandhi was not sure that the Congress was ready for such a difficult fight. But he at last agreed that if India had not become a dominion by 31st December 1929, the Congress would call for complete independence.

Gandhi knew that 1929 was going to be an important year and he spent a lot of time travelling around the country. There was some violence against the British that year and Gandhi could see that he needed to find a satyagraha campaign for people to follow. Young Indians wanted change and Gandhi had to find a way for them to fight for it peacefully.

In May 1929, a new Labour government took power in England, and in June, the British Viceroy, Lord Irwin, went to England for talks. When he returned in October, he told Indians that there would be a 'Round Table Conference' the next year for people from the British government and from British India and the princely states. The Simon Commission was sent home and Irwin said that India was looking towards becoming a dominion.

On 23rd December, Gandhi and other Indian leaders went to Delhi to meet with Lord Irwin. They wanted him to promise that India would become a dominion and that a new constitution[81] would be made at the Round Table Conference. But there were many in the British government who were against this and Irwin knew that he could not make the promise.

So at midnight on 31st December, as the New Year began, Congress members in Lahore put up the Congress flag and promised to fight for complete independence. They wanted Gandhi to decide how the fight would happen, but at first Gandhi had no ideas. 'I am thinking night and day,' he told his friend Rabindranath Tagore in January, 'and I do not see any light coming out of the darkness all around.'

Then in February 1930, Gandhi suddenly knew what

they had to do. The Indian people would start a satyagraha campaign about salt. Many people laughed at the idea at first. How could India use something as important as satyagraha to fight about something as unimportant as salt? But Gandhi was sure that he was right. Salt came in from the sea all around India, but under the British salt law, Indians could not collect or sell it without paying a very high tax. It was cheaper for Indians to buy salt from the British, though they also had to pay tax on that. The salt law taxed everybody – Hindus and Muslims, peasants and those who had no land. Everyone needed salt and the poor Indian working hard in the hot sun needed it more than anyone else.

On 12th March, Gandhi and more than seventy others from the Sabarmati Ashram began to walk to Dandi, two hundred miles away. They walked for twenty-four days, stopping in villages where Gandhi spoke to the people. He told them to spin their own cloth, not to drink alcohol, and, when the time was right, to break the salt law. Many people from the villages joined the marchers, and when Gandhi reached the sea at Dandi on 5th April, there were thousands of people with him. Early the next morning, Gandhi went into the sea and picked up some salt in his hand. He had broken the law.

India had waited for this satyagraha for a long time. Hundreds of thousands of Indians went to the beach to make salt, drying it in dishes in the sun. Many people were arrested and the police were often violent, hitting satyagrahis. By the end of April, thousands of people were in prison, and Jawaharlal Nehru, the president of the Congress, and two of Gandhi's sons, Ramdas and Devadas, had also been arrested. But the campaign did not stop.

In Bihar, tens of thousands of people marched out of the city to make salt, and in Karachi, fifty thousand people watched while salt was made on the beach. In other parts of India, peasants stopped paying rent and land tax. Women

People breaking the salt laws, Bombay, 1930

demonstrated in the streets and people stood outside shops to stop anyone buying alcohol and foreign cloth. There was almost no violence, but more than sixty thousand satyagrahis were arrested for breaking the salt law.

Gandhi now decided that he and his marchers would attack the depot at Dharasana, where the British government kept its salt. But on 4th May, policemen came to arrest Gandhi in the middle of the night at Karadi, where he was camping with other marchers, and he was put in prison without trial. The marchers were without the leader they loved, but nothing could stop them now.

On 21ˢᵗ May, they made the attack at Dharasana. About 2,500 satyagrahis moved quietly towards the salt depot. When policemen told them to stop, they kept moving and at once the policemen came forward. They hit the satyagrahis on their heads and shoulders with lathis – heavy metal-ended sticks – and many of them fell to the ground, but not one of them fought back. The satyagrahis could see that they might be injured or killed, but they marched forwards without stopping. In the end, four died and more than a thousand were injured.

There were international reporters at Dharasana that day and the world soon heard what had happened. The satyagrahis had not taken very much salt, but they had shown the world that the British Raj treated Indian people cruelly[82] and unfairly. They had also shown, and learnt for themselves, that they had the power to free themselves from British rule.

10

An Invitation to London

Gandhi was, as always, very happy in prison, where he was allowed to spin and write non-political letters. But for Lord Irwin, Gandhi's arrest made life impossible. Indians were angry and ready to fight, and in some parts of the country they fought against the Raj, taking power from the British. The British Prime Minister, Ramsay MacDonald, had called for Indian independence, and he too wanted the problems in India to end.

On 26ᵗʰ January 1931, Irwin released Gandhi, Jawaharlal Nehru, Motilal Nehru and other Congress leaders from prison. Gandhi wrote to Lord Irwin asking if they could meet and on 17ᵗʰ February, they began talks. Gandhi and Irwin met in the Viceroy's new palace and their talks went on for sixteen days. On 5th March, the Irwin-Gandhi Pact was signed[83]. Gandhi agreed to stop the civil disobedience campaign and he promised that the Congress would come to the second Round Table Conference in London in the autumn. (The Congress had refused to go to the first conference in 1930 and it had been cancelled.) The Raj agreed to release everyone who had gone to prison for civil disobedience and it also now allowed Indians to make salt without paying high taxes.

When they heard about the pact, some Indians were disappointed because there was no promise of independence or dominion status for India. But many felt that with the release from prison of tens of thousands of people, India had won a great fight. They believed that the pact showed equality between Britain and India and between the Viceroy and Gandhi.

On 29th August, Gandhi sailed from Bombay for the Round Table Conference in England. He arrived in London on the 12th September and was met by crowds of people. While he was in London, he stayed in a community centre[84] in the East End, a poor area of the city. It was a long journey to and from his meetings in central London and he often arrived back late at night. But he wanted to live among poor people, and in the mornings, he enjoyed walking near the community centre and talking to the men and women of the East End.

It was autumn in England when Gandhi arrived, but he wore his usual loincloth with more cloths around him to keep him warm. He dressed like this when he went to Buckingham Palace to have tea with King George V and Queen Mary. After this meeting, someone asked him if he had had enough clothes on. 'The King had enough clothes for both of us!' Gandhi replied.

Charlie Chaplin, the famous film actor, asked to see Gandhi. Gandhi also met General Smuts, his old enemy-turned-friend

Gandhi meeting poor people in Bow, East London, 1931

from South Africa, Lord Irwin and hundreds of others. He spoke to the London Vegetarian Society, where he had been a member forty years earlier, and gave many other talks. He visited some famous universities and schools, answered many letters and gave many interviews. He was so busy that he only slept for about four hours a night while he was in London.

Gandhi also went to Lancashire to meet textile workers. For many of them, life had become harder when Indians stopped buying foreign cloth. Some had lost their jobs. But here, like everywhere he went in England, Gandhi helped people to understand what was happening in India. He was always ready to talk to people and because he was honest and kind, he made friends everywhere.

Gandhi won the hearts and minds^p of the British people, but the Round Table Conference did not go well. The British had invited representatives from the princely states, and also Anglo-Indians, Christians, Hindus, Muslims, Untouchables and Parsis. All these representatives wanted a separate electorate – they wanted their national, religious or caste group to have seats[85] in government that only people from that group could vote for.

Gandhi was strongly against this. Anyone wanting to divide India in this way did not understand the country, he said. India was already too divided. Gandhi wanted a new independent India where Indians voted for Indians, and where religion and caste became unimportant in politics. He believed that India would only win independence if Hindus, Muslims, Untouchables and all the other groups worked together.

There was no plan for Indian independence at the Round Table Conference, and Gandhi could see that British ministers – under their new government – were ready to come down hard^p on any campaign against the Raj. 'I came looking for peace,' Gandhi said as he left England in December, 'but I am going back afraid of war.'

Stopping in Switzerland and Italy, Gandhi arrived home in India on 28th December. The friends who met him in Bombay had bad news. Jawaharlal Nehru and others from the Congress had been arrested, and because Indians in some parts of the country were refusing to pay rent, the government had made special new laws. The police were now allowed to arrest people and put them in prison without trial, take their homes and money, and stop peaceful demonstrations.

Gandhi asked the new British Viceroy, Lord Willingdon, for a meeting and told him that the Congress would fight against these new laws. But on 3rd January 1932, Gandhi himself was arrested and taken once more to Yeravda Prison. All Congress organizations were closed and almost all Congress leaders were put in prison. Indians fought against the Raj's special new laws, but Willingdon believed he could bring peace to India quickly with a hard handᵖ. In January and February 1932, about seventy-five thousand Indians were arrested and hundreds of thousands were hit with lathis. It was the strongest and cruellest drive against Indian people since the mutiny of 1857.

11

A Fast to Death

On 17th August 1932, while he was still in prison, Gandhi learnt that the British Prime Minister, Ramsay MacDonald, had decided to give the Untouchables a separate electorate in Britain's new constitution for India. Gandhi believed that this would make the division between the Untouchables and other Hindus stronger than ever. The next day, he wrote to MacDonald and told him that he would fast to death against this decision, beginning on 20th September.

At first, Gandhi did not tell any other people about his promise to fast to death. So when the news came out, on 12ᵗʰ September, people in Britain and India were extremely worried. At meetings all across India, people asked Gandhi not to fast. Thousands of letters arrived at Yeravda Prison and at the Viceroy's house, and political leaders across India did everything they could to stop Gandhi's fast. But at half-past eleven on 20ᵗʰ September, Gandhi took his last meal of lemon juice and honey with hot water.

Something extraordinary[86] now happened in India. Gandhi had said that if Hindus were not ready to turn away from the idea of Untouchability, they should let him die. But Gandhi was the people's Mahatma and they were not going to lose him. The day before Gandhi started his fast, twelve temples in Allahabad allowed Untouchables to pray there for the first time. Every day after that, more temples opened their doors to Untouchables, and all over India, Hindus and Untouchables ate meals together and met in streets and temples. Letters arrived at Yeravda from organizations in villages, towns and cities across India which now promised to treat Untouchables equally. Untouchables were allowed to walk on roads that had been closed to them and they shared benches and water wells with caste Hindus for the first time. Suddenly India was moving forward once more.

While ordinary Indians threw away the prejudices of a lifetime to save their Mahatma, political leaders went to work too. On 20ᵗʰ September, in Bombay, important Hindu leaders met with Bhimrao Ambedkar, the Untouchables' representative, who wanted to keep the separate electorate for them. Ambedkar, an Untouchable who had become a lawyer, believed that Untouchables would not feel safe talking about the way they were treated by Hindus if they were elected by both Hindus and Untouchables. The Hindu leaders could understand this and they now needed to find an agreement that would help with this problem and make Gandhi happy. And of course the British government had to agree to it too.

Sir Tej Sapru, one of the important Hindu leaders, had a clever plan which Ambedkar felt might work. The idea was to keep the Hindu and Untouchable electorate together, but to protect some seats for the Untouchables. Sapru and other leaders travelled through the night to explain their plan to Gandhi, who asked to meet with Ambedkar. On 22nd September, Ambedkar came to Yeravda, where Gandhi lay on a bed in the prison garden, under a mango tree, with his books and writing paper. The talks went well, but Gandhi was already very weak[87] and ill, and on the 23rd, his doctors warned that he could die at any moment.

More meetings between Ambedkar and the Hindu leaders brought them close to an agreement on Sapru's idea, and finally, on 24th September, the fifth day of Gandhi's fast, the Yeravda Pact was signed. On the 25th it was passed at a conference in Bombay. But the pact meant nothing if Ramsay MacDonald did not agree to it too. It was now Sunday in England, and when the words of the pact were sent through to London, MacDonald and his ministers were out of the city. Gandhi's friends in London did everything they could to get a quick reply, and MacDonald came back to London quickly and looked at the pact with his ministers until midnight on Sunday night.

Gandhi was now very close to death, and on the morning of Monday 26th September, his great friend Tagore came to the prison to sing songs to him. Then, at last, news came from London: the British government agreed to the Yeravda Pact. At 5.15 that afternoon, Gandhi broke his fast with a glass of orange juice and many of his friends and followers cried as they watched.

A few days after the end of the fast, Gandhi was already stronger and was able to spin once more. He had done something

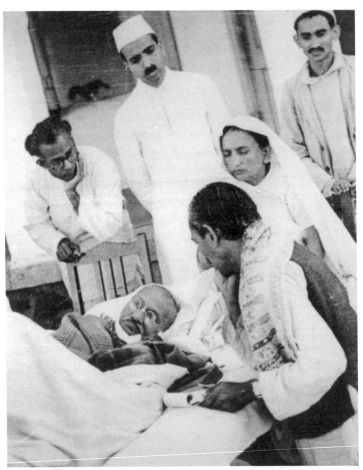

Gandhi fasting

extraordinary. Untouchability had not gone completely, but Gandhi had changed Hindu society forever. Untouchables still had the worst jobs and were still at the bottom of society, but people now understood that prejudice against them was wrong and the 'Harijans' had a chance to be free at last.

12

Into War

When Gandhi decided to fast again in May 1933, this time for his own health and happiness, the British released him from prison. They were worried that another fast would kill him and they did not want him to die in prison.

The civil disobedience campaign had started up again during Gandhi's time in prison. When he was released, Gandhi asked for a meeting with Lord Willingdon to try to bring peace back to India, but Willingdon did not want to meet. Gandhi decided to march with Kasturbai and a group of ashramites towards the village of Ras in Kheda, where many peasants had lost their land. He was arrested with the others, but released a few days later and told to stay in Poona. When he left Poona, he was arrested again and told that he would go to prison for a year. He fasted once more and was released from prison, but this time he decided to move away from politics and work for the Harijans for the rest of the year.

That year, Gandhi and his followers left the Sabarmati Ashram. Gandhi was worried that the government would take the ashram, and in September he moved to Wardha, near Nagpur. From there, in November, he went travelling around India once more, writing for his new weekly publication, the *Harijan*, and visiting and collecting money for Harijans.

In August 1934, he resigned[88] from the Congress, and, at his wish[89], Jawaharlal Nehru became president of the party once more. Gandhi told his friends in the party that he was ready to come back and help when he was needed and its leaders still came to him when they had to make important decisions. For example, he told the Congress that they should stop campaigning for swaraj with civil disobedience for a time.

Nehru was disappointed by this, but Gandhi told him that the fight was not over. This was just a quiet time before it began once more.

In 1935, the Act of India gave the country a new constitution. The act did not give Indians self-government, but it did promise elections in which thirty-five million people could vote and these were held early in 1937. Gandhi agreed that Congress members should enter the elections, because he hoped that they would be able to organize the country ready for independence. The Congress won the 1937 elections in six provinces – or areas – of India. But as the party took power, the Muslim League began to turn against it. The Muslim League had not done as well as it had hoped in the elections, and the leader, Jinnah, now believed that the Congress had become a party for Hindus only.

Subhas Chandra Bose became president of the Congress in 1938 and Gandhi did not like his leadership, because Bose wanted the Indian people to use violence against the Raj. Gandhi's ideas of peace and non-violence had become stronger with time. During the Boer War and the First World War, he had asked Indians to fight for Britain. But early in 1939, as the Second World War came close, Gandhi felt differently. On 3rd September, Britain went to war against Germany. Without speaking to the Congress, Lord Linlithgow, who had become Viceroy in 1936, said that India was at war too. A Working Committee of the Congress met in Wardha and at this meeting, it became clear that Gandhi had very different ideas from the rest of the party. Gandhi wanted Indians to help Britain in the war, but he did not want them to fight or to fight back if India was invaded[90]. The Congress wanted India to fight for Britain, but only if she was given her independence.

While Gandhi did not agree with these ideas, he was happy to speak for the Congress and he met Lord Linlithgow several times at the end of 1939. But the Viceroy's answer was always the same. There would be changes after the war, but he could not promise independence. In June 1940, the Working Committee in Wardha went against Gandhi for the first time and decided that it could not agree with him about non-violence. On 7th July, the Congress made the Rajaji Agreement. If India was given complete independence, she would fight with Britain in the war.

But Winston Churchill was now Prime Minister of Britain and he had always been against Indian independence. He believed that Britain was at its best in the nineteenth century when the British Empire was growing. India, for him, kept that time alive. So in August 1940, Linlithgow told the Congress that Britain, having controlled India for so many years, could not let her go now. He also said that Britain could not give power to an Indian government that many people in the country did not agree with. Britain had begun to listen to Jinnah and his Muslim League, who now had new ideas. Angry with the 'Hindu Congress', many Muslims now believed that there could never be one India. They wanted a separate country for Muslims.

The Congress had been ready to fight for Britain, but they now felt completely powerless. They agreed with Gandhi to start a new, controlled civil disobedience campaign that would not give Britain too many problems while it was fighting the war. One by one, members of the Congress made speeches or wrote against the war and were arrested. By the end of 1941, nearly twenty-five thousand people had been put in prison.

In December 1941, Japan attacked American ships at Pearl Harbour. America now came into the war, fighting with Britain and her allies, who declared war on Japan. Suddenly the war had come to Asia and the allies now needed India's help. President Roosevelt of the United States of America and members of the Labour party in Churchill's wartime government asked Churchill to talk to India about independence. In March 1942

Churchill sent Sir Stafford Cripps to Delhi. Cripps brought with him some plans from the British government and for three weeks he talked with India's important political leaders.

Under the plans, India would become a dominion after the war and Indians would make their own constitution and govern the country. But one third of the members of the new government would be chosen by Indian princes, who were very close to Britain. This, many thought, would allow Britain to keep controlling India. Gandhi and Jinnah were also against the plans because they would allow any province to become independent. Gandhi was worried that this would divide India into Hindu India, Muslim India and Princely India. For Jinnah, the plans did not give Muslims the separate country that they wanted. Cripps' plans also asked Indians to fight if the country was invaded, but under Britain's leadership – and the Congress did not want such control. On 12th April, therefore, Cripps went home to Britain. The Congress, the Muslim League and other Indian political organizations had all rejected[91] his plans.

13

Quit India!

By June 1942, Indians were even more angry and frightened. The Japanese had invaded Burma and were now very close. Indians were ready to fight, but Britain would not give them the power to do anything. Some Indians had now turned against the British and were ready to fight for Japan. Would India now become a place where Japan fought against the British and Indians fought against each other? Gandhi felt that everything he had worked for was in danger.

He had to do something and he thought of a simple idea.

Gandhi and his people would ask Britain to leave India. On 8th August 1942, the Congress agreed to the idea of 'Quit India' and prepared a resolution[92] for the British government. 'British rule must end at once,' the resolution began. If British rule ended, the Indian government would fight against a Japanese invasion, by non-violence or with guns, and would allow allied forces into India. But if British rule did not end, the Congress would begin a campaign of civil disobedience.

That night, Gandhi and many other Congress leaders were arrested, and the next morning, the Congress was banned. At once, India rose up in rebellion[p]. All around the country, there were demonstrations. Post offices, police stations and government buildings were burnt down, and some Raj officials were killed. Telephone wires were cut and bridges were blown up. More than one hundred thousand Indian nationalists were arrested. They had been ready for violence and Gandhi's arrest set that violence free.

Gandhi wrote angrily to the Viceroy. Why was he arrested before he had called for civil disobedience to start? Lord Linlithgow believed that Gandhi and the Congress had called for the violent rebellion of August 1942, but Gandhi told him that the British government had made it happen. The government had made the people of India mad with anger, Gandhi said, and the arrests had started the rebellion. How could the Viceroy say that he had called for this violence when he had worked for non-violence all his life? Furious, Gandhi decided to fast. He fasted for thirteen days, but the British refused to release him from prison. On 2nd March 1943, when he was close to death, Kasturbai gave him orange juice and his health slowly improved. He was now seventy-three years old.

This was just the start of a very difficult time for Gandhi. Kasturbai – or Ba (Mother) as everyone called her – was also taken to prison the night after Gandhi's arrest, after she had said she would speak at a meeting. She was with Gandhi at

Aga Khan Palace, where she found life very hard. 'Why do you ask the English to quit India?' she asked him after their arrest. 'Our country is big enough. We can all live here.'

There were also happy times between them in prison. Gandhi gave Kasturbai lessons every day, trying to teach her about the geography of India and to improve her reading and writing. In the evenings they sat and sang songs together. But by December 1943, Kasturbai was very ill and doctors said there was nothing they could do. The government allowed her sons and grandsons to visit, which made her happy. On 22nd February 1944, Kasturbai died in Gandhi's arms. She and Gandhi had been together for sixty-two years and many people loved her and looked up to her. It was a sad time for Gandhi, who later said of his wife, 'It is because of her that I am today what I am.'

Gandhi with his wife Kasturbai

14

Towards Independence

By June 1944, it was clear that the allied forces would soon win the war. Gandhi now felt sure that India could win her independence and he wanted agreement between the Congress and the Muslim League. In July, Gandhi wrote to Jinnah. They met several times in September, but then talks broke down. Jinnah wanted partition – he wanted the areas of India where there were more Muslims than Hindus to become a separate country, Pakistan. Gandhi agreed that people in those areas could vote to decide on partition, but he wanted India to win her freedom first. Jinnah wanted partition now, while the British were still in India, and he wanted only Muslims to vote for it.

In June 1945, Lord Wavell, India's new Viceroy, released several important political leaders who had been in prison since August 1942. He also invited India's leaders to a meeting that month and promised a new council. There would be an equal number of Hindus and Muslims, and an equal number of Congress members and Muslim League members on the new council. These would be chosen by Wavell from lists the parties gave him. The Congress was a much bigger organization than the Muslim League, so this did not seem fair to Congress members. But they wanted Wavell's plan to work so much that they agreed to it.

Jinnah did not want the plan to work. He said that he wanted to choose all the Muslims in the council. But this would mean that the Congress could not suggest any of the many Muslims in their party, including their new president, Azad. Also, the Congress was a national and non-religious organization. It would be wrong for them to choose only Hindu members. The talks came to an end.

In July, a new Labour government was elected in Britain. The war in Europe had ended in May, and in August, Japan stopped fighting too. The Labour government and Lord Wavell called for elections in India that winter, after which a new constitution would be agreed for an independent India. In the elections of December 1945, the Congress won most of the non-Muslim seats and the Muslim League most of the Muslim ones.

In March 1946, a group of British ministers arrived to decide how India's new national government would work. They also needed to decide if Britain should give Jinnah the separate Pakistan he asked for. In May, after long talks with India's political leaders, the ministers published their plan. They could understand why Muslims were worried about living with Hindus under Indian rule, the ministers said. There were many more Hindus than Muslims in India and Muslims were worried that their religion and way of life would not be safe.

But in three of the provinces that Jinnah wanted to take into Pakistan, there were many Hindus. Life would be just as difficult for these Hindus, the ministers argued. If they made Pakistan smaller, so that it included only the areas where Muslims lived, the three provinces, each with their own languages, histories and traditions, would be divided. India, the ministers decided, should stay as one country. But India's new government would only be able to make decisions if the Hindus and Muslims agreed.

Jinnah was not happy about many parts of the plan, but he agreed to it. The Congress talked for a long time before agreeing to the plan. They were not happy about the way members were going to be chosen for the new government which would run India. Jinnah believed that the British would now ask him to become Prime Minister. But when the Congress at last agreed to the plan, Jawaharlal Nehru, who was president of the party once more, was asked to become Prime Minister of India.

Jinnah, furious, refused to have any role in the new government. The Muslim League called for a 'Direct Action Day' on 16th August, and there were violent riots[93] in Calcutta, in which hundreds of Hindus were killed. Over the next few days, Hindus fought back and even more Muslims died. Violence moved across India into the Punjab, Bengal and Bihar.

When Gandhi heard that Hindu-Muslim violence was moving from the cities into the villages, he felt that he had to do something. Gandhi decided to visit the Noakhali area of Bengal, which had seen terrible violence. Noakhali was far away in the east of India and many kilometres from the nearest city. When he arrived, he sent his followers to live alone in the villages, where they taught the people to live without violence. From November 1946 until March 1947, seventy-seven-year-old Gandhi moved from village to village. He stayed for two or three days in each village, talking and praying, then walked without shoes to the next one, four or five kilometres away.

As he travelled around the area, more and more people came to Gandhi's meetings and many Hindus who had run away from their homes began to come back. When Gandhi left Noakhali, he had not stopped the disagreements completely, but Hindus and Muslims were coming together more and more. Gandhi asked a Muslim and a Hindu in each village to keep its people safe.

Gandhi now moved to Bihar, where there had been terrible riots and more than five thousand people, mainly Muslims, had died. Gandhi visited Muslims who had lost family or their homes, and he collected money for them at his meetings. Many Muslims had run away from the area, and Gandhi called on Hindus to welcome them back and make them feel safe.

Gandhi had been in Bihar for three weeks when Lord Mountbatten, India's new Viceroy, asked him to come to Delhi. The British government had said that Britain would leave

India before June 1948, but Jinnah was still refusing to join the group that needed to make the constitution for independent India. Lord Mountbatten now wanted Jinnah and Gandhi to find an agreement that would give India a peaceful future as a free country.

15

Partition

In his talks with Mountbatten, Jinnah warned that there would be war between Hindus and Muslims if India was not partitioned. He wanted Pakistan to include all of the Punjab and Bengal, but Mountbatten could see that this was impossible. Gandhi did not want any kind of partition. In June 1947, Mountbatten told India that the people of Bengal, Punjab and Assam would vote on partition. If most people wanted partition, these three provinces would be divided, with one part in India and one part in Pakistan. The Congress, worried about losing its promised independence and about a war between Hindus and Muslims, went against Gandhi and agreed with Mountbatten's plan. The partition was soon official. India and Pakistan would become separate, independent countries in August that year.

Disappointed, Gandhi returned to Bihar after his meetings with Mountbatten. He wanted to show people that Hindus and Muslims could live in peace and that India did not need partition. In Bihar, there was some good news. Muslims were going back to their villages, with help from Hindus and Sikhs. If peace began to come back to the villages, Gandhi believed, then it would soon come in the cities and across the country.

On 9[94]th August 1947, Gandhi went to Calcutta, where rioting and violence had not stopped since Direct Action Day in 1946. When people saw Gandhi in the streets of the city, the anger between Muslims and Hindus died down[94]. Large crowds came to his prayer meetings every day and after the 14th August, there was a break in the violence.

When Independence Day came on 15th August, there were fireworks and great speeches in Delhi, but Gandhi spent the day quietly, spinning, praying and fasting. India was now divided into the Indian Union and the dominion of Pakistan. Because of this, independence was no longer the great change for India that Gandhi had hoped and worked for for so long.

But partition did not bring an end to the violence. Another fight between Hindus and Muslims broke out on the night of 31st August in Calcutta and Gandhi decided to fast to death. He wanted an end to the violence and he did not break his fast for three days, until Hindus, Muslims, Christians and city leaders promised that there would be no more fighting.

On 7th September, Gandhi left Calcutta and went to Delhi, where he found rioting in the city. Millions of Hindus and Sikhs had begun to move away from Pakistan, where Muslims were attacking them. And millions of Muslims were escaping from the Indian Union, where Hindus and Sikhs were attacking them. Over the next few months, more than fifteen million people left their homes and walked hundreds of kilometres to places where they had no work and nowhere to live. In the crowds there was hunger and illness, and many people died.

When escaping Hindus and Sikhs reached Delhi, many of these refugees[95] had to stay in dirty refugee camps outside the city. Gandhi walked across Delhi many times each day, speaking to the people and visiting the camps. He told people to keep clean, to share their food and to live for others as well as themselves. He asked people to bring blankets for the refugees as the nights became colder. At his prayer meeting

Refugees travelling to India and Pakistan during partition, October 1947

every evening, Gandhi asked the people if he could read from the Koran. He wanted them to understand and live with the religions of others.

Gandhi had helped to stop the terrible attacks and he wanted to go and help the Hindus and Sikhs in Pakistan, but could not do this until Muslims were living safely in India. Hindus had taken Muslims' homes from them in Delhi and many wanted all the Muslims to leave. How could Gandhi be sure that the attacks would not start again? He could not watch while Hindus, Muslims and Sikhs broke their new countries apart. So on 13th January 1948, Gandhi began his last fast to death.

On the first day of the fast, Gandhi walked to his prayer meeting as usual. But he became weak very quickly. On the third day of the fast, he lay on a bed outside Birla house, where he was staying in Delhi. His eyes were closed and there was khadi cloth around his face. Long lines of people walked past to see him and many cried as they prayed.

From the first day of the fast, Dr Prasad, the new president of the Congress, had organized meetings with people from different groups and organizations in Delhi. He hoped to find a real peace that would stop Gandhi's fast. On 18th January, Prasad came to see Gandhi with more than a hundred representatives from the city. Hindus, Muslims, Sikhs, Jews and Christians, together with representatives from the police and from all Delhi's important organizations, had signed a promise that there would be no more violence in Delhi. They promised that Muslims could move around Delhi freely and mosques that had been taken from them would be returned.

Were these things really true, Gandhi asked, or were people just trying to stop his fast? Would violence go on in other parts of India and Pakistan or would these representatives work to stop fighting between religious groups across the countries? They promised that they would. At last, when Gandhi was sure he could believe them, he broke his fast and drank some orange juice.

Gandhi had always said that he wanted to live until he was 125 years old. If they could keep their promise, he told the representatives, he would now make that wish once more. He would live that long, working for his people. Gandhi's fast brought a new hope for friendship. It had stopped religious riots and violence not just in Delhi, but across India and Pakistan.

16

To Rama

In the twelve days following the fast, Gandhi was very happy and he soon felt ready to go to Pakistan. Plans were made for him to travel there at the beginning of February. Gandhi was now seventy-eight years old, but his mind was still quick and brilliant and he had no problem working long hard days. India now loved him more than ever. Around the world, too, people could see that Gandhi was a great and special leader, and an extraordinary man. But on 20th January 1948, someone threw a bomb[96] at Birla House. A prayer meeting was going on when the bomb went off and people were very frightened. But no one was injured and Gandhi, not knowing until later what had happened, was not worried.

Friday 30th January began like any other day[p] for Gandhi. He got up at half past three in the morning, said his prayers, and then worked on a speech for a Congress meeting. He had a bath and some breakfast, and then slept for a short time. He talked with Delhi's Muslim leaders, and in the afternoon, lay in the sun while the newspapers were read to him. He saw visitors, did some spinning, and after dinner he left for his prayer meeting a little later than usual.

As he walked to the prayer meeting, he had on each side of him one of his younger cousins. He walked with an arm on each girl's shoulder, as he often did. When the three of them arrived at the prayer meeting, a man moved towards Gandhi. Gandhi's cousin thought the man wanted to kiss Gandhi's feet and she asked him to move away because they were already late. But the man pushed her away, pulled out a gun and shot Gandhi three times. 'Hey Rama,' (Oh God) Gandhi said quietly as he fell to the ground.

Gandhi was carried to Birla House and a doctor came after just ten minutes, but he was already dead. Gandhi's followers and friends could not believe what had happened and they sat next to his body crying. Then Prime Minister Nehru arrived. He hid his face in Gandhi's blood-covered clothes and cried like a child[P]. Later, on the radio, he spoke to the Indian people.

'The light has gone out of our lives,' he said, 'and there is darkness everywhere. The leader we loved, Bapu as we called him, is no more.'

The man who shot Gandhi, Nathuram Godse, hated non-violence and the charkha. He thought that Gandhi had made India and Hindu society weak. He was executed – killed for his crime – against the wishes of Gandhi's sons, Manilal and Ramdas.

Around the world, people shared in the deep sadness of India at the loss of the great leader the country had loved so much. On 31st January 1948, Gandhi's body was washed, covered in flowers and taken away for cremation[97]. One and a half million people marched to the cremation ground, and another million watched as 'Bapu' was taken past. Two weeks later, following Hindu tradition, Gandhi's ashes were taken to Allahabad by train. At every station, hundreds of thousands of people came to say goodbye to their Mahatma, praying and throwing flowers onto the train. And when at last his ashes were set free in the holy Ganges and Jumna Rivers, thousands more went into the water to be close to their great leader for the last time.

A year after the Mahatma's death, the Indian government set up the Gandhi Peace Prize, which in the year 2000 was given to Nelson Mandela*. Mandela had campaigned to win freedom for black people in South Africa, the country where satyagraha had first begun.

The Macmillan Biography Nelson Mandela *is now available. See the Macmillan Readers catalogue or visit www.macmillanenglish.com/readers for more information.*

Crowds at Gandhi's cremation, 1948

Today, Gandhi is remembered every year with a national holiday, Gandhi Jayanti, on the day of his birthday. He was not a political or religious leader, but he had an extraordinary power to make people follow him. He showed that non-violence was a great and strong force for change, and his ideas about satyagraha have been used by others fighting for freedom around the world. Gandhi gave his life to help the people of India. He lived in love, peace and truth, and his beliefs still continue to change people's lives.

Points for Understanding

1

1   What was the British Raj?
2   What were the four main groups in the Indian caste system and what jobs did they do?
3   Who were the Untouchables and what jobs did they do?
4   What was the name of the political party started by educated Indians in 1885?

2

1   Why was Mohandas Gandhi's father an unusual member of the Vaishya caste?
2   How did Mohandas learn about people of different religions when he was at high school?
3   Why could Mohandas not become a doctor?
4   How old was Mohandas when he got married?
5   What three vows did Mohandas make before he went to London?

3

1   How did Gandhi's vegetarianism change in London?
2   What did Gandhi try to learn in London to make himself into an 'English gentleman'?
3   What terrible news did he hear when he arrived back in India?
4   Why did Gandhi go to South Africa?

4

1   Why were so many Indians living in South Africa from the 1860s?
2   What happened to Gandhi on his journey from Durban to Pretoria?
3   Who was the Russian writer whose ideas interested Gandhi very much and what were his ideas?
4   Why did Gandhi not sail back to India after his year in Pretoria?

5

1 What did Gandhi and the Indian people do during the Boer War?
2 What important change did Gandhi make to his life after reading a book by John Ruskin in 1903?
3 At a meeting in Johannesburg in 1906, what did nearly three thousand people promise to do?
4 Why did nearly two thousand Indians burn their passes in Johannesburg in August 1908?
5 How did satyagrahi disobey the Black Act?
6 Why did Gandhi cancel the January 1914 march?

6

1 What did Gandhi change about his clothes when he arrived back in India?
2 When did Gandhi set up the Sabarmati Ashram and what was it?
3 What did Gandhi call the Untouchables and what did this word mean?
4 Why did Gandhi fast in March 1918?
5 How did satyagraha help the peasants of Kheda?

7

1 Under the new Rowlatt Act, for what could Indians be arrested without trial?
2 What is khadi, and why did Gandhi want people to start making it?
3 What was the picture on the new flag of the Indian National Congress?
4 Why were Mondays special for Gandhi?
5 Why did Gandhi cancel the campaign of civil disobedience in February 1922?

8

1 Why was Gandhi released from prison in February 1924?
2 How long did Gandhi fast for in September 1924 and why?
3 What did the people at the Sabarmati Ashram call Gandhi and why?
4 Why were Indian people angry about the Simon Commission?

9

1 Where did India's first civil disobedience campaign happen in 1928?
2 What did Gandhi decide that India's satyagraha campaign in 1930 should be about?
3 Why did Gandhi break the law when he picked up salt on 6th April?
4 What did satyagrahis do at Dharasana on 21st May?

10

1 What did Gandhi promise the British government under the Irwin-Gandhi Pact?
2 Where did Gandhi stay while he was in England?
3 What did Gandhi wear when he went to visit the King and Queen?
4 Why did Gandhi disagree with the other representatives at the Round Table Conference?

11

1 Why did Gandhi decide to fast to death in September 1932?
2 How did temples in Allahabad change when Gandhi began his fast?
3 What was the name of the agreement which stopped Gandhi's fast and what was the idea behind it?
4 How did Gandhi break his fast?

12

1 Why was Gandhi released from prison in 1933?
2 Which party did best in the elections of 1937?
3 Why were members of the Congress arrested again in 1941?

13

1 What did the Congress's 'Quit India' resolution say?
2 Why was there a rebellion in August 1942?
3 What sad event happened in Gandhi's family in 1944?

14

1 How did Jinnah hope that partition would divide India?
2 What was the problem with making a small Pakistan that included only the areas where Muslims lived?
3 Who was asked to become Prime Minister of the new government of India?
4 What did the Muslim League do because of this?
5 What did Gandhi want to teach people in the villages of Noakhali?

15

1 Which provinces of India would be divided under partition?
2 How many people left their homes because of partition?
3 Why did Gandhi decide to fast to death in January 1948?
4 Why did Gandhi stop his fast?

16

1 Who was with Gandhi when he was shot?
2 Who told the Indian people over the radio that Gandhi had died?
3 Where were Gandhi's ashes taken?
4 Who won the Gandhi Peace Prize in the year 2000?

Glossary

1 **ruled** – *to rule* (page 7)
   to officially control a country. *Rule* is the person, group or country that officially controls a place.

2 **government** (page 7)
   the people who control a country or area and make decisions about its laws and taxes. If people control a country or areas, they *govern* it.

3 **Emperor** (page 7)
   a man who rules an *empire* – a number of countries that are controlled by one person

4 **silk** (page 7)
   a thin smooth cloth made from the fibres produced by insects called *silkworms*

5 **power** (page 7)
   control of a country or government

6 **take control** – *to take control of something* (page 7)
   control is the power to make decisions about what happens in a situation. If someone *takes control*, they begin to use this power.

7 **colony** (page 8)
   a country that is controlled by another country

8 **tax** (page 8)
   an amount of money that you have to pay to the government. The money is used for providing public services and for paying for government institutions.

9 **peasant** (page 8)
   a poor person who works on another person's farm or on their own small farm

10 **law court** (page 8)
   a place where *law cases* – legal matters – and trials take place and are officially judged. Someone whose job is to make decisions in a *law court* is called a *judge*.

11 **divided** – *to divide something* (page 8)
   to separate people or things into groups or parts. The process of separating people or things into groups is called *division*.

12 **forced** – *to force someone or something* (page 8)
   to make someone do something that they do not want to do

13 **society** (page 8)
   people in general living together in organized communities, with laws and traditions controlling the way that they behave

14 **leader** (page 9)
   someone who is in charge of a group, organization or country
15 **political** (page 9)
   relating to *politics* – the ideas and activities that are involved in
   getting power in an area or governing it. Someone who has a job in
   politics is called a *politician*.
16 **conditions** (page 9)
   the situation or environment in which someone lives
17 **lawyer** (page 10)
   someone whose job is to provide people with legal advice and
   services. A *lawyer* who is allowed to speak in the higher law courts
   is called a *barrister*.
18 **independence** (page 10)
   freedom from control by another country or organization
19 **brave** (page 11)
   able to deal with danger, pain or trouble without being frightened
   or worried
20 **sensible** (page 11)
   reasonable and practical
21 **prayed** – *to pray* (page 11)
   to speak to God or a saint, for example to give thanks or ask for
   help. The practice of speaking to God is called *prayer*.
22 **shy** (page 11)
   nervous and embarrassed in the company of other people, especially
   people who you do not know
23 **snake** (page 11)
   a long thin animal with no legs and a smooth skin
24 **official** (page 11)
   someone with an important position in an organization
25 **peacefully** (page 11)
   in a way that does not involve war or violence
26 **Jain** (page 12)
   relating to a very old type of Hinduism which does not have a God
   but believes that people should have great respect for all living
   things
27 **tradition** (page 12)
   a very old custom, belief or story
28 **allowed** – *to allow someone to do something* (page 12)
   to give someone permission to do something or have something
29 **suffered** – *to suffer* (page 12)
   to experience something very unpleasant or painful

30 **moved** – *to move someone* (page 12)
to affect someone emotionally, especially by making them feel sad and serious

31 **procession** (page 12)
a line of people or vehicles that move in a slow formal way as part of an event

32 **care** – *to care for someone* (page 13)
to do the necessary things for someone who needs help or protection

33 **vow** (page 13)
a serious promise

34 **monk** (page 13)
a man who lives in a religious community away from other people

35 **committee** (page 16)
a group of people who represent a larger group or organization and are chosen to do a particular job

36 **publication** (page 16)
a magazine, newspaper or book. If you produce many copies of a magazine, newspaper or book for people to buy, you *publish* it.

37 **servant** (page 17)
someone whose job is to cook, clean or do other work in someone else's home

38 **indentured** (page 18)
forced by a contract to work for an employer for a fixed period of time. This period is called an *indenture*.

39 **prejudice** (page 18)
an unreasonable negative opinion or feeling, especially the feeling of not liking a particular group of people

40 **vote** – *to vote* (page 19)
to decide something, or to choose a representative or winner, by officially stating your choice, for example in an election

41 **set up** – *to set something up* (page 20)
to start something such as a business, organization or institution

42 **furious** (page 20)
extremely angry

43 **treated** – *to treat someone* (page 21)
to behave towards someone in a particular way

44 **dispensary** (page 22)
a place where you can get medicines and drugs

45 **medal** (page 23)
a round flat piece of metal that you are given for winning a competition or for doing something that is very brave

46 **carry** – *to carry something* (page 24)
to have something with you, usually in your pocket

47 **fine** (page 24)
an amount of money that you must pay because you have broken the law

48 **obey** – *to obey someone or something* (page 24)
to do what a person, rule or law says that you must do. Behaviour in which you refuse to obey orders or rules is called *disobedience*.

49 **repeal** – *to repeal something* (page 25)
to officially end a law

50 **dominion** (page 26)
an area that is ruled by one person or government

51 **Prime Minister** (page 26)
the political leader in countries that are governed by a parliament

52 **immigration** (page 26)
the process in which people enter a country in order to live there permanently

53 **miner** (page 26)
someone whose job is to dig coal and other substances from a *mine* – a large hole or tunnel in the ground from which people take coal, gold etc

54 **strike** (page 26)
a period of time during which people refuse to work, as a protest

55 **march** – *to march* (page 26)
to walk to a place as part of an organized group protesting about something

56 **cancel** – *to cancel something* (page 26)
to say that something that has been arranged will not now happen

57 **campaign** (page 27)
a series of actions that are intended to achieve something such as social or political change

58 **right** (page 27)
something that you are legally or morally allowed to do or have

59 **disappointed** (page 28)
unhappy because something did not happen or because someone or something was not as good as you expected

60 **spin** – *to spin* (page 30)
to twist fibres into thread to make cloth. You *weave* the fibres –
cross the fibres over and under each other on a special machine – to
make cloth. Types of woven cloth are called *textiles*.

61 **rented** – *to rent something* (page 31)
to pay money regularly to use a house, room or land etc that
belongs to someone else

62 **demonstrated** – *to demonstrate* (page 31)
to protest about something in a public place. An occasion when
people protest in this way is called a *demonstration*, and people who
demonstrate are called *demonstrators*.

63 **mill** (page 31)
a factory where a product such as cotton, wool or steel is made

64 **ruined** – *to ruin something* (page 32)
to spoil or destroy something

65 **crop** (page 32)
a plant that is grown for food

66 **Secretary of State** (page 32)
the politician in charge of a particular government department in
the UK

67 **arrested** – *to arrest someone* (page 32)
if the police *arrest* someone, they take that person to a police
station because they think that he or she has committed a crime

68 **trial** (page 32)
the process of examining a case in a court of law and deciding
whether someone is guilty of a crime

69 **shooting** – *to shoot* (page 33)
to fire a gun

70 **investigation** (page 33)
the process of trying to find out all the facts about something in
order to discover who or what caused it or how it happened

71 **ally** (page 34)
a country that makes an agreement to help another country,
especially in a war. The *Allied Forces* were the countries that united
to fight in the First and Second World Wars.

72 **election** (page 35)
an occasion when people vote for, or *elect*, someone to represent
them, especially in a government. The people who vote in an
election are called the *electorate*.

73 *representative* (page 35)
someone who has been chosen by a person or group to vote, speak or make decisions for them
74 *charged* – *to charge someone with something* (page 36)
to accuse someone of committing a crime
75 *penalty* (page 36)
a punishment for breaking a rule or law
76 *appendicitis* (page 37)
an illness in which a small tube in your body near your stomach, called your *appendix*, becomes infected and has to be removed
77 *release* – *to release someone* (page 37)
to let someone leave a place where they have been kept
78 *equality* (page 38)
the state of being *equal* – having the same rights, status and opportunities as other people
79 *wrist* (page 40)
the part of your body that joins your hand to your arm
80 *increased* – *to increase something* (page 41)
to make something become larger in number or amount
81 *constitution* (page 42)
a set of basic laws or rules that control how a country is governed or how it operates
82 *cruelly* (page 45)
in a way that causes pain to people or animals or makes them unhappy
83 *signed* – *to sign something* (page 46)
to write your name on something in order to show that you have written it or that you agree with what is written on it. A *pact* is an agreement between two or more people or organizations in which they promise to do something.
84 *community centre* (page 46)
a building used by the people who live in an area for meetings, social events and other activities
85 *seat* (page 48)
a position as a member of a parliament or committee
86 *extraordinary* (page 50)
very unusual and surprising
87 *weak* (page 51)
lacking physical strength or good health

88 **resigned** – *to resign from something* (page 53)
   to state formally that you are leaving your job or position
89 **wish** (page 53)
   a feeling that you want something or want to do something
90 **invaded** – *to invade something* (page 54)
   to take or send an army into another country in order to get control
   of it. An occasion when this happens is called an *invasion*.
91 **rejected** – *to reject something* (page 56)
   to not accept or agree with something such as an offer or an
   argument
92 **resolution** (page 57)
   a formal proposal that is considered by an organization and then
   voted on
93 **riot** (page 61)
   a violent protest by a crowd of people
94 **died down** – *to die down* (page 63)
   if something *dies down*, it becomes much less noisy, powerful or
   active
95 **refugee** (page 63)
   someone who leaves their country because of a war or other
   threatening event
96 **bomb** (page 66)
   a weapon that is made to explode at a particular time or when it
   hits something
97 **cremation** (page 67)
   the process of burning the body of a dead person. The substance
   that remains after a person's body has been cremated is called their
   ashes.

Useful Phrases

do what they were told – *to do what you are told* (page 7)
to obey someone

make him into – *to make someone into something* (page 15)
to give someone the right qualities for a particular job, purpose, etc.

won the hearts and minds – *to win the hearts and minds of someone*
(page 48)
to make people love you and agree with your opinions and share your
beliefs

come down hard – *to come down hard on someone* (page 48)
to criticize or punish someone severely

with a hard hand (page 49)
in a way that is strict or extreme

rose up in rebellion – *to rise up in rebellion* (page 57)
to start to protest and fight against a government or leader

began like any other day – *to begin like any other day* (page 66)
used to say that the morning was a typical morning with all the usual
events and activities

cried like a child – *to cry like a child* (page 67)
to have a lot of tears coming from your eyes because you are very sad or
hurt

Glossary and Useful Phrases definitions adapted from Macmillan Essential Dictionary
© *Macmillan Publishers Limited 2003* www.macmillandictionary.com

Exercises

Background Information

Match the names to the descriptions.

1 The British Empire __G__
2 The British East India Company ....
3 Portugal and the Dutch Republic ....
4 The Raj ....
5 The Brahmins, the Kshatriyas, the Vaishyas and the Shudras ....
6 The Untouchables ....
7 Hindus and Muslims ....
8 Bengali, Marathi, Hindustani ....
9 The Viceroy ....
10 The Indian National Congress ....

A the countries which lost control of parts of India to the British in the early seventeenth century
B the main Hindu castes into which Indians were born
C an Indian political party which first wanted more rights for Indians to govern their country and finally independence for India
D some of the main languages spoken in India
E the British ruler in India whilst it was a colony
F the time of British rule in India
G countries and lands outside Britain which were ruled by Britain
H the group of people considered to be the lowest in Indian society and who lived and worked in awful conditions
I a trading organization which gained power and control of much of India
J the two biggest religious groups in India

Multiple Choice

Tick the best answer.

1 Who paid for Gandhi to go to London to study law?

   a His mother.

   b His father.

   c His brother.   ✓

   d His wife's family.

2 Which of the following is NOT true of Gandhi's family life?

   a His first child died soon after it was born.

   b He got married at the age of thirteen.

   c He sent his children to England to give them a good education.

   d His eldest son wrote articles attacking him.

3 In which country did Gandhi first go to prison?

   a South Africa.

   b England.

   c India.

   d Pakistan.

4 What was the name for Gandhi's form of peaceful, non-violent protest?

   a Swaraj.

   b Satyagraha.

   c Ashram.

   d Kasturbai.

5 Who gave Gandhi the name Mahatma?

   a His parents.

   b His friend, the writer and poet, Rabindranath Tagore.

   c The peasants of Kheda.

   d His eldest son.

6 Which of the following did Gandhi NOT work and fight for in his life?

   a To improve the lives and rights of the Untouchables.

   b To free India's peasants from their poor, uneducated lives.

   c To achieve the partition of Pakistan from India.

   d To make India independent from Britain.

Vocabulary: Verbs and nouns

Match a verb and noun to make phrases from the biography.

1	obey		the fight
2	spin		the law
3	put on		land
4	sign		articles
5	win		a pact
6	take		a white suit
7	rent		cloth
8	write		a vow

Now choose a phrase to complete the sentences below, changing the tense or form of the verbs where necessary. Each phrase may only be used once.

1 As a form of peaceful protest, Gandhi's followers promised that they would not _____*obey the law*_____ which said they had to carry a pass.

2 Before going to London, Gandhi _____ that he would not touch wine, women or meat.

3 When he arrived in England, Gandhi _____ , but found no-one else was dressed like him.

4 Whilst in London, Gandhi _____ for the London Vegetarian Society's publication *The Vegetarian*.

5 In the Himalayas poor peasants _____ from the British and were treated very badly by them.

6 Gandhi believed that _____ was a good way to bring together all types of people and organize them for civil disobedience.

7 Gandhi believed that the Indians would _____ for independence by being honest and peaceful rather than violent.

8 The British Prime Minister, Ramsay MacDonald, finally _____ which stopped Gandhi's fast to death.

84

Vocabulary: Adjectives

Write the letters in the correct order to make adjectives that complete the sentences.

1. Gandhi's mother was a very EILUROSIG _religious_ woman who prayed before every meal and went to the temple daily.

2. Gandhi believed that it was important not to tell lies nor break a promise. He told his followers to always be NEOTHS ....

3. Gandhi's childhood friend Methab told Gandhi that he was RABEV .... and unafraid because he ate meat.

4. Gandhi grew up in a EUUDRLTC .... family surrounded by books and music.

5. As a young boy, Gandhi had been very HSY .... , but as he got older he spoke to others and made good friends easily.

6. Gandhi's mother was a NSIESLEB .... woman who always thought carefully and tried to do the right thing.

7. When he was young, Gandhi was EDFIGTEHRN .... of ghosts, robbers and snakes, unlike his wife.

8. Gandhi felt TIYULG .... for telling lies to his parents when he was eating meat.

9. Gandhi was XICTDEE .... about getting married because of the special clothes and processions.

10. When Gandhi arrived in London, he missed his family and was terribly OMSIECHK .... for India.

11. Gandhi was FOIRUSU .... when the Viceroy accused him of causing a violent rebellion because he had always wanted non-violence.

12. When an Untouchable family first came to live in the ashram, many people were KDESOCH ....

Useful Phrases

Match the sentence halves 1–5 with A–E to make full sentences.

1   When Gandhi and other Congress leaders were arrested, India rose
    __C__
2   Gandhi won the hearts ....
3   In London Gandhi tried to learn good English, but this did not make

    ....
4   At the London Round Table Conference, Gandhi saw that the British
    would come ....
5   On seeing Gandhi's blood-covered clothes after his shooting, Nehru
    cried ....

A   down hard on any protest in India against British rule.
B   like a child.
C   up in rebellion, with thousands more arrested for violent protest.
D   him into an English gentleman and he realized it never would.
E   and minds of people everywhere he went.

Grammar: Infinitives of purpose

Match the sentence halves 1–6 with A–F to make full sentences.

1   Gandhi went to London   __C__
2   Gandhi's family had painted their home in Rajkot ....
3   Gandhi stayed in South Africa ....
4   Gandhi encouraged Indians to spin cloth ....
5   When he returned to London, Gandhi stayed in a community centre in
    the East End ....
6   Gandhi said he would fast to death ....

A   to fight against a law that would take away the vote of Indians in Natal.
B   to live among poorer people.
C   to study law and become a barrister.
D   to welcome him home from London as a qualified barrister.
E   to bring people together and make them ready and organized for civil
    disobedience.
F   to protest against the idea of dividing the electorate.

Grammar: Past perfect

Complete the sentences using the past perfect form of the verb in brackets.

1 The Dutch and the British took land from the black South Africans after they _____ (arrive) there in the seventeenth century.

2 Previously Gandhi _____ (be) vegetarian because of his mother's beliefs, but in London he started to believe in vegetarianism for himself.

3 The Indians were angry that after they _____ (help) Britain during the war, they still did not get independence.

4 Gandhi _____ (not want) Pakistan to be partitioned from India, but he could not stop this happening.

Grammar: Rights, obligations and ability

Rewrite the sentences using the words given.

1 Mohandas' family were not allowed to eat or touch meat.
could
Mohandas' family _____ *could not eat or touch meat* _____ .

2 Putlibai told her children they must not touch the Untouchables.
allowed
Putlibai told her children they _____ .

3 Gandhi could not find work when he returned to India.
able
Gandhi _____ .

4 Any Indian carrying a seditious paper was made to go to prison for two years.
had
Any Indian carrying a seditious paper _____ .

5 Gandhi said that Indians had to be peaceful and honest to get what they wanted.
must
Gandhi said that Indians _____ .

Macmillan Education
The Macmillan Building
4 Crinan Street
London N1 9XW
A division of Macmillan Publishers Limited
Companies and representatives throughout the world

ISBN 978–0–2304–0838–8
ISBN 978–0–2304–0869–2 (with CD edition)

First published 2011
Text © Macmillan Publishers Limited 2011
Design and illustration © Macmillan Publishers Limited 2011

Illustrated by Peter Harper
Cover photograph provided by **Corbis**/Bettmann

The authors and publishers would like to thank the following for permission
to reproduce their photographic material:
AKG Images/Ullstein Bild p52(t); **Alamy**/Dinodia Images pp26(t), 29,
39(b), 58(b); **Corbis**/Bettmann p64(t); **Getty Images**/Margaret Bourke-
White/Time & Life Pictures p68, Getty/ Henry Guttmann p15(b),
Getty/Hulton Archive p44(t), Getty/Keystone p21(t), Getty/Popperfoto
pp9(t),47; **Topham Picturepoint**/Topfoto.co.uk p34(t).

Every effort has been made to trace copyright holders, but if any have
been inadvertently overlooked the publishers will be pleased to make the
necessary arrangements at the first opportunity.

Printed and bound in Thailand

without CD edition
2020   2019   2018   2017
11   10   9   8   7   6   5

with CD edition
2016   2015   2014   2013   2012
10   9   8   7   6   5   4   3   2